CW00938475

Soho Theatre Company
and Olivia Wingate Productions presents

dirty butterfly

by debbie tucker green

First performed at Soho Theatre on 26 February 2003

This production has been made possible by a
TIF/SOLT New Producers Bursary financed by
The Society of London Theatre and supported by
the Arts Council of England, the Mackintosh Foundation,
Clear Channel Entertainment U.K and the Equity Trust Fund.

Soho Theatre is supported by

Soho Theatre Company has the support of the
Pearson Playwrights' Scheme, sponsored by Pearson Plc

Performances in the Lorenz Auditorium
Registered Charity No: 267234

dirty butterfly

by debbie tucker green

Sharon Duncan-Brewster	AMELIA
Jo McInnes	JO
Mark Theodore	JASON

Director	Rufus Norris
Assistant Director	Rachael Claire Lovett
Designer	Katrina Lindsay
Lighting Designer	Nigel Edwards
Sound Designer	Paul Arditti

Production Manager	Nick Ferguson
Stage Manager	Ros Terry
Deputy Stage Manager	Dani Youngman
Chief Technician	Nick Blount
Production Electrician	Adrian Peterkin
Scenery built & painted by	Robert Knight

*Soho Theatre Company and Olivia Wingate Productions
would like to thank*
Loukia Minetou, Dorothy Rowe, Theatre Investment Fund

Press Representation
Martin Shippen at Soho Theatre (020 7478 0142)

Advertising: Haymarket

Graphic Design: Jane Harper

Casting: Amy Bell

Soho Theatre and Writers' Centre
21 Dean St, London W1D 3NE

Admin: 020 7287 5060 *Fax:* 020 7287 5061 *Box Office:* 020 7478 0100
www.sohotheatre.com   *email:* box@sohotheatre.com

Biographies

Cast

Sharon Duncan-Brewster, *Amelia*

Sharon's theatre credits include *Peepshow* (Frantic Assembly at Lyric, Hammersmith); *Keepers* (Hampstead Theatre); *So Special* (Royal Exchange, Manchester) *Crave* (Paines Plough); *Yard Gal* (MCC Theatre on Broadway/ Cleanbreak/Royal Court Theatre); *No Boys Cricket Club* (Theatre Royal, Stratford East); *Ashes and Sand* and *Babies* (Royal Court). Film credits include *Body Story* (Redstar) and *Christmas* (Channel4/World Pictures). Sharon's television credits include *Maisie Raine*; *Backup*; *Hope I Die Before I Get Old*; *The Bill*; *Baby Father* and *Bad Girls*.

Jo McInnes, *Jo*

Jo's theatre credits include *Uncle Vanya*, *The Herbal Bed*, *The General From America* and *As You Like It* (RSC); *Bluebird* and *4:48 Psychosis* (Royal Court); *The Children's Hour* (National Theatre); *Edward II* (Crucible Theatre) *Biloxi Blues*, *The Importance Of Being Earnest*, *Private*

Lives, *Wait Until Dark*, *Memoirs Of A Survivor*, *Billy Liar* (Salisbury Playhouse) and most recently, *Inland Sea* (Oxford Stage Company). Jo's film credits include *Gangster No. 1*, *Birthday Girl*, *Brown Paper Bag* and *My Wife Is An Actress*. Radio credits include *Night On The Town*, *Scars* and *Uncertainty* (BBC Radio 4). Jo recently established the theatre company A.P.E. and directed her first play called *Tape* (New Venture Theatre, Brighton). Television credits include *Playing The Field* and *Soldier Soldier*.

Mark Theodore, *Jason*

Theatre credits include *Rumblefish* (World Stage Premiere and National Tour for Pilot Theatre Co); *A Bitter Herb* (Theatre Royal Bristol Old Vic); *Edmond and The Collection* (Northern Stage Ensemble) and *Measure for Measure* (RNT). Television credits include *Casualty* (BBC); *The Bill* (Pearson) and *Queer as Folk* (Red Productions). Film credits include *Ali G in da House* (Working Title) and *NOD* (Bart Productions).

Company

Debbie Tucker Green,
Writer

Theatre, *born bad* (currently short listed for Susan Smith Blackburn award, new Hampstead theatre) directed by Kathy Burke, to premiere April '03 and *two women* (Paines Plough theatre company at Soho Theatre). Radio, *freefall* (BBC Radio 3, finalist for Prix Europa Award 2002, currently nominated for a Sony award) and *to swallow* (BBC Radio 4, to be broadcast June '03).

Katrina Lindsay, *Designer*

Katrina Lindsay studied at Central, St Martins School of Art and Design. Design credits include *Sleeping Beauty* (Young Vic), *Tall Stories* (The Shout, BAC/Vienna Festival, Long Wharf Theatre, Connecticut); *Under the Blue Sky* (Royal Court); *Measles* (The Gate) and *Our Boys* (Soho Theatre). With Rufus Norris she is joint artistic director of Wink, designing *Strike Gently*, *The People Downstairs*, *the art of random whistling* (Young Vic Studio); *Waking Beauty*, *Rosa Carnivora* and *The Lizzie Play* (Arts Threshold, UK tours and Hong Kong). Opera work includes *La Cenerentola* (ETO); *The Magic Flute* (Holland Park) and *Carmen* (Mid Wales Opera). Television credits include *The Power of Genius* (animated trailer for documentary on Picasso for Channel 4); *Fugee Girl* (costumes, C4) and *Metrosexuality* (short listed for a BAFTA for Production Design on this C4 six-part series).

Paul Arditti,
Sound Designer

Paul has designed for most of the significant theatre directors of the last twenty years. As well as his extensive freelance work in the West End, RSC, around the UK and on Broadway, Paul spent three years designing at the National Theatre and eight as Head of Sound at the Royal Court Theatre 1993-2002. Recent work includes *Accidental Death of An Anarchist* (currently at the Donmar); *My Brilliant Divorce* and *Auntie and Me* (currently in the West End); *Twelfth Night* and *Uncle Vanya* (Donmar, and currently at the Brooklyn Academy of Music, NY); *Far Away* (Royal Court/ West End / New York Theatre Workshop); *Sleeping Beauty* and *Afore Night Come* (directed by Rufus Norris at the Young Vic); *Homebody/ Kabul* (Young Vic / Cheek By Jowl); *Plasticine* (Royal Court); *The People Are Friendly* (Royal Court); *The Night Heron* (Royal Court) and *Romeo and Juliet* (Chichester). Paul was nominated for a Drama Desk Award for Complicite's production of *The Chairs* on Broadway, and won the Drama Desk Award for Outstanding Sound Design in 1992 for the music theatre piece *Four*

Baboons Adoring the Sun (Broadway).

Rufus Norris, *Director*

Recent theatre includes *Sleeping Beauty, Afore Night Come* (Young Vic); *Small Change* (Sheffield Crucible) and *Mish Alla Ruman,* a comedy in Arabic about the Intifada (Al Kasaba Theatre in Ramallah, Palestine). Music-theatre work includes *Tall Stories* (BAC, Vienna Festival) and *Sea Tongue* (Huddersfield Contemporary Music Festival) with The Shout, as well as *Pierrot* by Orlando Gough and writing the libretto *for On Thee We Feed,* composed by Richard Chew (ENO Baylis Programme). Productions of other plays include *Under The Blue Sky; About The Boy, Clubbed Out* (Royal Court), *My Dad's Cornershop* (Birmingham Rep), *Two Women* and *Dirty Butterfly* (Soho Theatre lunchtimes), *Small Craft Warnings* (Pleasance, London) and *The Measles* (Gate). Rufus is co-artistic director of Wink, for whom he has directed *Strike Gently Away From Body, The People Downstairs* and *the art of random whistling* (Young Vic Studio), *Rosa Carnivora* and

The Lizzie Play (Arts Threshold, national tours, Hong Kong). Rufus was given the Outstanding Newcomer Award at the Evening Standard Awards 2001 for *Afore Night Come,* and was awarded an Arts Foundation Fellowship this year. Rufus is also Associate Director at the Young Vic.

Nigel Edwards, *Lighting Designer*

Theatre lighting designs include *The Oresteia* (Royal National Theatre); four productions for the Royal Shakespeare Company; *The Maids* (Young Vic); three plays by Sarah Kane (London, Berlin, Spain and Dublin); two productions in 2001 at the West Yorkshire Playhouse; five productions for Paines Plough as well as productions at the Almeida, the Royal Court, Soho Theatre, Actors Touring Company, Lip Service and the National Theatre of Macedonia. Nigel has designed and toured extensively for Forced Entertainment, The Right Size and Tottering Bipeds. Nigel Edwards has designed the lighting for productions at the Welsh National Opera and the Lyric Hammersmith. He made his Opera North debut in 2001.

Olivia Wingate Productions

Olivia Wingate Productions is a commercial theatre production company devoted to the nurturing and cross-fertilising of new playwrights both in London and New York. OWP works very closely with many playwrights, directors and subsidized/Not-For-Profit theatre companies with the aim of improving their profile within the theatre industry on both sides of the Atlantic. OWP was established by Olivia Wingate in August 2002, after her lengthy involvement with numerous theatres and production companies both in London and New York.

For further information about OWP please visit our website: www.owproductions.co.uk

● soho
● theatre + writers' centre

Soho Theatre Company

Soho is passionate in its commitment to new writing, producing a year-round programme of bold, original and accessible new plays - many of them from first-time playwrights.

'a foundry for new talent . . . one of the country's leading producer's of new writing' Evening Standard

Soho aims to be the first port of call for the emerging writer and is the only theatre to combine the process of production with the process of development. The unique Writers' Centre invites writers at any stage of their career to submit scripts and receives, reads and reports on over 2,000 per year. In addition to the national Verity Bargate Award – a competition aimed at new writers – it runs an extensive series of programmes from the innovative Under 11's Scheme, Young Writers Group (14-25s) and Westminster Prize (encouraging local writers) to a comprehensive Workshop Programme and Writers' Attachment Scheme working to develop writers not just in the theatre but also for radio, TV and film.

'a creative hotbed . . . not only the making of theatre but the cradle for new screenplay and television scripts' The Times

Contemporary, comfortable, air-conditioned and accessible, the Soho Theatre is busy from early morning to late at night. Alongside the production of new plays, it's also an intimate venue to see leading comedians from the UK and US in an eclectic programme mixing emerging new talent with established names. Soho Theatre is home to Café Lazeez, serving delicious Indian fusion dishes downstairs or, upstairs, a lively, late bar with a 1am licence.

'London's coolest theatre by a mile' Midweek

Soho Theatre Company is developing its work outside of the building, producing in Edinburgh and on tour in the UK whilst expanding the scope of its work with writers. It hosts the annual Soho Writers' Festival – now in its third year which brings together innovative practitioners from the creative industries with writers working in theatre, film, TV, radio, literature and poetry. Our programme aims to challenge, entertain and inspire writers and audiences from all backgrounds.

Soho Theatre and Writers' Centre
21 Dean St, London W1D 3NE

Admin: 020 7287 5060   *Box Office:* 020 7478 0100

● soho
● theatre + writers' centre

Bars and Restaurant

Café Lazeez brasserie serves Indian-fusion dishes until 12pm. Late bar open until 1am. The Gordon's Terrace serves Gordons and Tonic and a range of soft drinks and wine.

Email information list

For regular programme updates and offers, join our free email information list by emailing box@sohotheatre.com

If you would like to make any comments about any of the productions seen at Soho Theatre, why not visit our chatroom at www.sohotheatre.com?

Hiring the theatre

Soho Theatre has a range of rooms and spaces for hire. Please contact the theatre managers on 020 7287 5060 or email hires@sohotheatre.com for further details.

Soho Theatre Company

Artistic Director: Abigail Morris
Assistant to Artistic Director:
    Sarah Addison
Administrative Producer:
    Mark Godfrey
Assistant to Administrative
    Producer: Tim Whitehead
Literary Manager: Ruth Little
Literary Officer: Jo Ingham
Associate Director:
    Jonathan Lloyd
Associate Director: Tessa Walker
Casting Director: Ginny Schiller
Development and Marketing
    Director: Zoe Reed
Development Officer: Gayle Rogers
Marketing Officer: Ruth Waters
Press Officer: Martin Shippen
    (020 7478 0142)
General Manager:
    Catherine Thornborrow
Acting General Manager:
    Jacqui Gellman
Front of House and Building
    Manager: Anne Mosley
Financial Controller: Kevin Dunn
Finance Officer: Hakim Oreagba
Box Office Manager:
    Kate Truefitt
Deputy Box Office Manager:
    Steve Lock
Box Office Assistant: Darren
    Batten, Wendy Buckland,
    Eleanor Lee, Bret McCallum,
    Leah Read, Natalie Worrall
    and Miranda Yates
Duty Managers: Morag Brownlie,
    Mike Owen and Kate Ryan
Front of House staff: Helene Le
    Bohec, Adam Buckles, Sharon
    Degan, Meg Fisher, Claire
    Fowler, Sioban Hyams, Grethe
    Jensen, Sam Laydon, Clair
    Randall, Katherine Smith,
    Rebecca Storey, Esme
    Sumsion, Luke Tebbutt, Claire
    Townend and Jamie Zubairi
Production Manager:
    Nick Ferguson
Chief Technician: Nick Blount
Technicians: Adrian Peterkin,
    Andrew Turner

Board of Directors and Members of the Company

David Aukin – chair
Cllr Robert Davis – vice chair
Nicholas Allott
Lisa Bryer
Tony Buckley
Tony Elliott
Barbara Follett MP
Norma Heyman
Bruce Hyman
Lynne Kirwin
Tony Marchant
Michael Naughton
David Pelham
Michael Pennington
Sue Robertson
Philippe Sands
Eric H Senat
Meera Syal
Marc Vlessing
Zoë Wanamaker
Sir Douglas Wass
Richard Wilson OBE
Roger Wingate

Honorary Patrons

Bob Hoskins *president*
Peter Brook CBE
Simon Callow
Sir Richard Eyre

Development Committee

Bruce Hyman – co chair
Catherine Fehler –co chair
Philippe Sands – vice chair
Nicholas Allott
David Aukin
Don Black OBE
David Day
Amanda Eliasch
Emma Freud
Madeleine Hamel
Marie Helvin
Norma Heyman
Cathy Ingram
Jonathan Lane
Lise Mayer
Michael Naughton
Barbara Stone
Richard Wilson OBE
Jeremy Zimmerman

The Soho Theatre Development Campaign

Soho Theatre Company receives core funding from Westminster City Council and London Arts. In order to provide as diverse a programme as possible and expand our audience development and outreach work, we rely upon additional support from trusts, foundations, individuals and corporates.

All of our major sponsors share a common commitment to developing new areas of activity and encouraging creative partnerships between business and the arts.

If you would like to find out more about supporting Soho Theatre, please contact Gayle Rogers, Development Officer on 020 7478 0111 or email gayle@sohotheatre.com.

We are immensely grateful for the invaluable support from our sponsors and donors and wish to thank them for their continued commitment.

Core sponsors **Bloomberg, TBWA\GGTDirect**

Research and Development Anon ● Calouste Gulbenkian Foundation ● The Samuel Goldwyn Foundation ● The Harold Hyam Wingate Foundation ● Really Useful Theatres

Education Anon ● Delfont Foundation ● The Fishmongers' Company ● Hyde Park Place Estate Charity ● International Asset Management ● JJ Gallagher Ltd ● Madeleine Hamel ● The Paul Hamlyn Foundation ● John Lyon's Charity ● Roger and Cecil Jospé ● Mathilda and Terence Kennedy Charitable Trust ● The Royal Victoria Hall Foundation ● St James's Trust ● The Kobler Trust

Access John Lewis Oxford Street

Production Esmée Fairbairn Foundation ● Linbury Trust ● Unity Theatre Trust

Individuals **Gold Patrons**: Anon ● Katie Bradford ● Julie & Robert Breckman ● David Day ● Raphael Djanogly ● John Drummond ● Jack and Linda Keenan ● **Silver Patrons**: Anon ● Rob Brooks ● **Bronze Patrons**: Richard Borchard ● Samuel French Ltd ● Solid Management ● Paul & Pat Zatz

Studio Seats Anon ● Jo Apted ● Peter Backhouse ● Leslie Bolsom ● Mrs Alan Campbell-Johnson ● David Day ● Raphael Djanogly ● Imtiaz and Susan Dossa ●Anthony Gardner ● Catherine Graham-Harrison and Nicholas Warren ● Sally A Graudons ● Hope Hardcastle ● Bruce Hyman ● Roger Jospé ● Jeremy Levison ● John and Jean McCaig ● Annie Parker ● Eric and Michèle Senat ● Simonetta Valentini ● Marc Vlessing

● soho
● theatre + writers' centre

In 1996, Soho Theatre Company was awarded an £8 million Lottery grant from the Arts Council of England to help create the Soho Theatre + Writers' Centre. An additional £2.6 million in matching funds was raised and over 500 donors supported the capital appeal. The full list of supporters is displayed on our website at www.sohotheatre.com/thanks.htm

Building Supporters   Supported by the Arts Council of England with National Lottery funds

The Lorenz Auditorium supported by Carol and Alan Lorenz

Principal Sponsor   Gettyimages

Rooms   Gordon's Terrace supported by Gordon's Gin ● The Education and Development Studio supported by the Foundation for Sport and the Arts ● Equity Trust Fund Green Room ● The Vicky Arenson Writers' Seminar Room ● Writers' Room supported by The Samuel Goldwyn Foundation ● Unity Theatre Writers' Room ● Writers' Room supported by Nick Hornby and Annette Lynton Mason ● The Marchpole Dressing Room ● Wardrobe supported by Angels the Costumiers ● The Peter Sontar Production Office ● The White Light Control Room ● The Strand Dimmer Room ● The Dennis Selinger Meeting Room

Building   The Esmée Fairbairn Foundation ● The Rose Foundation ● The Meckler Foundation ● Roberta Sacks

Soho First   BAFTA ● Cowboy Films Ltd ● Simons Muirhead & Burton

Gold Patrons   Eric Abraham ● Jill and Michael Barrington ● Roger Bramble ● Anthony and Elizabeth Bunker ● John Caird ● David and Pat Chipping ● John Cohen at Clintons ● Nadia and Mark Crandall ● David Day ● Michael and Maureen Edwards ● Charles Hart ● Hat Trick Productions ● David Huyton at Moore Stephens ● Miriam and Norman Hyams ● David Jackson at Pilcher Hershman ● The St James' Trust ● John Kelly–European Quality ● Mr and Mrs Philip Kingsley ● The McKenna Charitable Trust ● Nancy Meckler and David Aukin ● Michael and Mimi Naughton ● Robert Ogden CBE ● Diana Quick ● Christian Roberts ● Lyn Schlesinger ● Peter M Schlesinger ● Carl Teper ● Diana and Richard Toeman ● Richard Wilson OBE ● Margaret Wolfson

dirty butterfly

debbie tucker green

for Dona Daley
peace

thanks to the royal court, ruth little, caryl and my spars

Characters

AMELIA, *black*

JASON, *black*

JO, *white*

The audience should surround the actors.

*Prior to the Epilogue, the characters are always onstage;
their dialogue is always between each other and never to
the audience. / denotes where dialogue starts to overlap.
Throughout this section options can be taken regarding who is
talking to who and when, with varying implications for the
characters. The form of the piece has been left open for these
choices to be made.*

*Names appearing without dialogue indicate active silences
between characters listed.*

*Music track: 'Secret Place' by Jhelisa (from 12-inch, not
album version).*

JO, JASON *and* AMELIA *onstage.*

JO. Sorry . . . I'm sorry . . . sorry . . . sorry I'm sorry...

AMELIA *starts to sing, increasing her volume to try to drown out the repetitive sound of* JO.

JASON. Sssh.

They both stop.

Beat.

JO *picks up* AMELIA*'s melody.*

JO. Hmmm, you ever?

JASON (*to* AMELIA). You ever –

AMELIA (*to* JASON). you ever got that feelin –

JO. you ever –

AMELIA. got that restless kinda feelin?

JASON. You ever –

AMELIA. got that can't find somethin to match your mood kinda feelin – you ever got that, Jase?

JO. You ever –

JASON. found yourself doin somethin you can't help.

AMELIA. You ever –

JASON. gotcha self doin somethin you can't stop.

Beat.

'Meilia?

AMELIA. No.

JO. You ever woken up of a mornin wonderin this was gonna be your last? You ever got that feelin in your stomach as you lay there wonderin?

JASON. found yourself feelin that?

AMELIA. No.

JO. Like butterflies

Like butterflies gone ballistic.

Butterflies gone wrong.

JASON. You ever –

AMELIA. no once. Take it twice. *Nah*. I haven't.

JO. Woke up this morning like that I did, and lay there lookin across at him.

JASON. In my room I sit there listenin out for him n' all.

Me by myself – listening out. Hard for him – hard for her –

AMELIA. you're getting worse you are

JO. me looking up above us, layin there in our duvet over us – looking across at husband and wondering if this morning was gonna be my last.

AMELIA. You're getting worse you are.

JASON. And you're not?

Like you're normal.

AMELIA. Like you're a role model for it is it? You the logo for normality is it?

JO. Have a touch a mine.

AMELIA. You the name brand – I'm just the Primark, is it?

JO. Take a touch a mine.

AMELIA. Don't think so somehow.

See – how bout she lettin me get back to the normal that I know.

The mornins that I knew.

JO. –

AMELIA. How bout that then?

How bout her mornins not infringin on mine?

JO. It gets worse.

JASON. How bout her mornins not infringin on mine?

AMELIA. Xactly.

JO. It got worse.

AMELIA. Jase –

JO.ssshh.

AMELIA. You are getting worse.

You really are.

JASON. How bout you not sleepin on your sofa?

AMELIA. How bout you makin it to your bed?

JASON. How bout you makin it up your stairs –

AMELIA. how bout that then Jay?

JASON. You ever / tried doin what I –

AMELIA. My sofa ent no sofa bed. And my downstairs ent no bedroom. But I can sleep on it –

JO. is it?

AMELIA. sleep in it –

JO (*amused*). is it?

AMELIA. got used to it good.

JO. Ent you got a perfectly good bed up your stairs though?

Now, I'm sure you got a perfectly good bedroom up your stairs . . .

AMELIA. And I wash in my downstairs sink –

JASON. you don't have to

AMELIA. do my teeth in there an all.

JASON. You don't have to.

AMELIA. And you don't have to sit up there, be up there, Jason.

It's not compulsory.

JASON. Unlike the art a sleepin in your front room.

AMELIA.

JASON.

JO. Knew today had potential.

Knew that today was gonna kick.

Knew from the reluctant wakin, eye glue poppin, dead leg
stretchin of the meeting of the morning, that today – was
gonna kick.

Me it. Or it me. And I was up for it.

I was, was just . . . really / up for it.

AMELIA. Up that mornin – up *that* early – and before I'm out
Jase – before I *deliberately leave* to go out – I'm just in my
yard – in my front room – on my sofa – lookin me
somethin. DJ to do me a favour and play me somethin nice
on the f.m, on the downstairs radio – a 'don't-mind-what',
y'know. A 'don't mind me', y'know – somethin hollow
from the radio –

JO. you can singalong to. Great.

AMELIA. . . . Even before I'm up to wash.

I'm just looking me a – and my upstairs radio's left on in
the bathroom, talkin. And my only telly's upstairs in the
empty bedroom – on. But down here my batteries are dead.

JASON. I'm not lookin anything.

JO. Don't use his eyes much does he?

AMELIA. My batteries died a death. Leavin me listenin to
niche and my CD's idle.

JASON. I'm busy listening.

JO. He always will

JASON. She givin me summink to lissen to for free.

JO. I give the people what they want . . .

AMELIA. *My* CD's is idle – and I don't do silents – is it.

So.

Me tryin t'summon up su'un to sing – a tune that comes out
nice, nice to make me feel lovely – lovely makin me feel
special, specially me knowin that I'm not.

Aye Jase?

Am I Jase? . . .

Am I Jason?

How bout that then?

That's all I'm lookin.

I was lookin a tune, Jason.

JASON. I know.

AMELIA. This is my mornin.

JASON. I know.

AMELIA. And know that I'm down here not going up. In a mi own yard. Not goin up. How bout – not goin up.

Not goin up.

Not goin up.

JO. You said.

AMELIA. I'm not going up to hear –

JASON. Her.

AMELIA. *She*.

JO. I know.

AMELIA. Bleedin thru.

JO. I know.

AMELIA. A tune.

JASON. I know.

AMELIA. So I won't feel bad.

JASON. Then don't.

AMELIA. Don't feel bad.

JO. You won't.

AMELIA. Cos that's all I was doin.

JO. You said.

JASON. Tell her she's disturbing you.

AMELIA. I can hear y'know.

JASON. Tell her to leave you alone.

JO. Tell me then.

JASON. Tell her you can hear her.

AMELIA. Leave me alone.

JO *is amused.*

JASON. Tell her you can't sleep in your upstairs no more –

JO. c'mon then.

JASON. Tell her how she –

JO. I dare ya –

JASON. tell her –

JO. double dare ya –

JASON. tell her –

JO. *tell me then*.

AMELIA. I can't stand the wakin up to hearin you.

I can't stand you.

I can't stand the you and your him nex door to me.

You and your bad both a yers nex door to me – you and your bad – sex – nex to me – nex door to me, nex door to my bedroom.

I just can't stand the bad a that.

JO. Bad sex over bein bad minded.

AMELIA. Bad minded over havin bad taste.

JO. Bad taste over havin bad music –

AMELIA. there ent nuthin wrong with my music.

There ent nuthin wrong with my / music –

JO. y'music or y'voice?

AMELIA. Don't be tryinta dis my vocalality –

JO. skills.

AMELIA. You ever / try and cuss my –

JO (*mocking*). *You ever* / is it?

AMELIA. Fuck off Jo.

JO. . . . No.

Beat.

AMELIA. I walk to work.

JO. And.

AMELIA. Now, I walk to work.

JO. And?

AMELIA. Leave earlier than I have to.

JO. So?

AMELIA. Leave out while iss still dark.

JO. So what –

AMELIA. So! Today's got 'look at fuckin you' all over it.

JO. And?

AMELIA. Last night got 'look at you' all over it an all.

JO. So?

AMELIA. Last night got you and your 'extra-ness' messin it up from the start. You and your – 'what?' – givin it some from the get go.

JASON. Giving him some from the get go –

AMELIA. for a change.

JASON. First time for everything.

AMELIA. And there was no need for this mornin to be so damn extra and full up a you, Jo.

JO. But it *is* though Amelia.

AMELIA. *You* made it extra – see! You make it different, Jo, you let it get worse'n what it needs to be. You wanna hit back you make sure you win. You wanna play contender – you stay in the ring. Five minutes a your inspired fuckries last night –

JASON. and he ent gonna let her forget it this morning.

AMELIA. See, there was no need for today to be so . . . fucked.

JASON. There was no need – yes.

AMELIA. For you to be so . . . fucked.

JO. Is he sure about 'needs' / is he?

AMELIA. For you to be fuckin with us daily.

JASON. Yeh, iss like –

AMELIA. fuck.

JO. Looks like he's got a need of his own / don't it.

JASON. *Iss* like – wakin up with my back still up to it. On my /
    side.

JO (*dryly*). Looks like he's getting his needs met, Amelia.

    AMELIA *clocks* JO.

JASON. Hard up on it. On my side.

AMELIA. What?

JASON. It's like –

    waking up with my head on the crick – back up against it,
    legs lying in fronta me and the wall laughin like it won.
    Wall all triumphant it's had me against it all night as its
    trophy.

    Upstairs on my side a that wall that's what it's like.

AMELIA. You're getting worse, Jase.

JASON. That's my night.

AMELIA. See.

JASON. Body bitchin on me that sleeping upright on the 90
    degree ent a natural way to catch some zzz's. Thass my
    mornin.

AMELIA. Should go to your bed shouldn't yer.

JASON. –

AMELIA. Should go to your bed then – on your side.

JASON. what like you do on yourn?

AMELIA. Should –

JASON. go to my bed – like how you take to your sofa – is it?
    Like how you sleepin on your sofa is the example I should
    follow

AMELIA. y'should –

JASON. phone and say I'm strugglin so you, sofa lying – *on
    your side,* could struggle down the phone with me should I?

AMELIA. Phone's upstairs.

JASON. Shoulda phoned and had a one-to-one a strugglin
    together should I?

AMELIA. I left it upstairs

JASON. wouldn'ta rung then.

Beat.

AMELIA. And you didn't.

JASON. No.

AMELIA. And you don't.

JASON. No.

I sit up, up here on my side.

AMELIA. I lie down, down there on mine and down there I
can't hear.

JASON. Chicken shit – makes it cheating, then.

JO. Cheating?

AMELIA. I can't hear is good.

JO. He thinks this is a game?

JASON. You not hearin is easy, so that's your / night.

JO. Tell him this isn't a game / Amelia.

JASON. I heard –

AMELIA. me not hearin her and him is lettin my imagination
run a marathon, Jase, and that don't make it cheating and
that don't make it easy and that don't make me 'chicken
shit' –

JASON. makes you somethin. I *heard.*

AMELIA. And what you doin your side makes you somethin
an' all –

JASON. least I'm there.

JO. It's not / a game.

JASON. Least I'm up – and / I heard –

JO. tell him it's / not a game –

AMELIA. y'not meant to be there!

And I ent takin shit from you cos you should stop listening
– *your side* – you should step away – *your side.*

You should stop sittin there – should finish your hearing and
you should do like what I do on my side and gone to your
bed.

JASON. Sofa. Ain't it.

AMELIA. That's my night.

AMELIA.

JASON.

JASON. I shoulda gone to my b-b / (bed).

AMELIA. I know.

JASON. It's my own f-f- / (fault)

AMELIA. I know, Jason.

JASON. . . . But I hear her Amelia.

AMELIA. I don't wanna know that.

JO. . . . I do.

JASON. Last night –

JO. I did.

JASON. She hit back . . .

JO. I did.

AMELIA. See, so – how bout, Jo, you tryin t'mek the effort –

JO. I did.

AMELIA. some piece a effort to try to shut the fuck up?

   Bitecha lip or sumthin.

JO. He does that for me.

AMELIA. Holdja tongue.

JO. He does that for me an all.

AMELIA. Take it like a fuckin man / then –

JO. I do.

   Don't I.

JASON. She ever gonna / stop?

AMELIA. You ever / had to –

JO. you ever wanted – to piss?

   Beat.

AMELIA. no.

JO. Proper get the urge to power piss.

AMELIA. *No.*

JO. Got the ultimate – do it or die, have to go – piss?

AMELIA *glares coldly at* JO.

Hold it in for the longest time convincin yourself you don't really wanna – butcha got no choice an / haveta –

AMELIA. no I haven't.

JO. Has he ever had to piss like that?

AMELIA. He ain't.

JASON. Amelia.

JO. . . . You sure?

AMELIA. Have ya Jaye?

JASON. No.

AMELIA. See.

JO. Can't hold out – haveta go.

JASON. She shouldn't have gone.

AMELIA. I don't wanna know.

JO. Haveta go before it makes its own route outta me body.

JASON. Amelia –

JO. know I shouldn't go but I have to get up to – this mornin / I have to

AMELIA. I don't need to know, Jo

JO. If it don't come out as piss come out a yellow tears.

AMELIA. Jo.

JO. And I look beside me to / check –

JASON. *Amelia.*

JO. I sneak a peep, shift a touch, ease up –

JASON. from under.

JO. Ease out

JASON. from beside him

JO. and creep out

JASON. of their bed.

AMELIA. Jason.

JASON. She does –

JO. I do, Amelia.

JASON. I hear, Amelia.

JO. I hear him hearing . . .

    . . . I hear him hearing me hear.

    And he knows it.

    Beat.

    So. When last did you wanna piss like that, then..?

    JO *half laughs dryly.*

    Beat.

    Silence

    JASON *listens.*

    JO *smiles.*

AMELIA. Jason – Jason –

JASON. what?

AMELIA. Jason –

JASON. ssshhh . . .

    AMELIA *kisses her teeth.*

    Can still hear her and –

AMELIA. just sleep downstairs.

JASON. Can still –

AMELIA. sleep in your downstairs Jase.

JASON. I can –

AMELIA. shut her out and sleep downstairs or come over and
    sleep downstairs with me on my sofa at mine . . .

JASON. Can hear her even when he's done.

AMELIA. If you wanted.

JASON. Particularly when he's done doin her in –

AMELIA. Jason –

JASON. I sit / up –

AMELIA. know you're welcome –

JASON. I sit up back to the / wall –

AMELIA. know you're welcome if you're lookin / company

JASON. back to the wall ear to the glass

AMELIA. and company could do worse than me bein with you and how bout that then?

JASON. Sitting up, back to the wall, ear to the glass – stayin in to listen – stayin up to listen – staying up to listen in on her – and her man – from my side a the wall – again –

AMELIA. Jason.

JASON. I know.

I know.

AMELIA. Please.

JASON. This is my mornin –

AMELIA. I know you won't

JASON. and my mornin before –

AMELIA. know how long since I've had good company?

JO. Know how long since I've had good company?

JASON. But now, this morning – this mornin my body is proper feelin it and letting me know. This is / my morning.

AMELIA. I'd like your company . . .

Beat.

JO. Company a one and that's too much. Company a two and that makes trouble.

AMELIA. Jason.

JO. Head or tails, which one would you pick?

AMELIA. Jason?

Beat.

JO. Company a one and I do my own head in.

JASON. Company a two and he does it in for her.

AMELIA. And you beggin a third party to hear both that's what's sick.

JO. But you're 'downstairs' entcha. You're in your *downstairs* – entcha A-melia.

A-lone.

A-gain.

You've taken to your sofa, your side, while I'm still wantin with that painful morning piss that won't pass yeh. That I've got to get up to go to get rid of while I'm wonderin – no – *worryin* about wakin him up. *My side*.

AMELIA (*dryly*). Yeh. It's a worry.

JO. It is.

JASON. I'm worried about her.

AMELIA. Don't be.

JO. This is my mornin.

AMELIA. Definitely don't be.

Why dontcha just go, Jo?

JO. Go and he'll wake – or a lie there and it'll flow / kinda piss.

AMELIA. What-*evah*.

JASON. But she went

Amelia, she *went*.

AMELIA. Big deal.

JO. And it was like –

AMELIA. enough.

JO. Sorta like –

AMELIA. I'm off.

JO. Another morning like that.

JASON. You goin?

AMELIA. I'm off.

I'm off out.

I went.

To the caff.

Beat.

I went out to work.

You should've come with, Jason.

JASON. . . . I'm not goin nowhere

AMELIA.

JASON.

JO.

JO. Heard you the other side still, still trying not to be heard . . .

JASON. I won't go nowhere.

AMELIA. You shoulda come, Jase.

JO. But you've gone, Amelia.

You've got up, you've gone out and you have *left*.

. . . you ever –

JASON. you ever –

JO. You ever felt to piss like that then?

. . . Thought not.

AMELIA. . . . Melody, me and my shit. Me and my borin as ever shit.

Melody make what I'm doin go a little quicker, do what I'm doin quicker still –

bored doin what I'm doin – make me forget that I'm doin it.

Melody, me and my borin as ever, pickin up my bottom lip miserably moppin of the other people's floor – shit, Jase.

The being there being invisible – shit.

And radio land's lettin me down with all their songs sounding like shit and it's doin me in, doing my head right in and maybe what you're hearin, Jaye, maybe what you're hearin where you're at is better'n what I am.

Beat.

JASON. It's a quiet morning thru' the flimsy walls, after a lively night a activity.

JO. Can't hold out haveta go.

JASON. It's a quiet mornin thru' the flimsy walls after a lively night a the usual –

JO. fuckin

JASON. usual

JO. fighting

JASON. unusual fighting back – and I – I can't ... I c-c-can't ...

> JO *winces.*

> JASON *listens.*

AMELIA. Don't.

> *Beat.*

> Don't Jase.

JASON. . . . She's on her hands and knees –

JO. . . .

JASON. She's nervous as she crawls . . .

JO. Mmm. (JO *nods.*)

AMELIA. Drama queen.

JASON. Him hard breathin it –

JO. *that's* right.

JASON. But she don't breathe –

JO. yeh.

JASON. Cos she won't breathe –

JO. yes.

JASON. Iss like she can't breathe and I hear –

AMELIA. don't Jase.

JASON. I hear him roll back over as you –

JO. draw the door closed behind me?

> Well done.

AMELIA (*dryly*). Well done.

You made it to the bog. Big deal.

JO. You know what Amelia. It is.

JASON. Hear what 'Meil, I'm still sittin there as I was from the night before. I'm still sittin in the same position against that same wall. Shit'd be funny if it wasn't shit eh?

JO. There's a word for people like you.

AMELIA. Word for people like her but she don't use it.

JO. Bucket.

Squeeze.

Swipe.

AMELIA. Dawn turns to mornin proper –

JO. why don't you call yourself a cleaner? How come you don't call yourself a – not even 'domestic assistant', 'facilities hygienist' –

AMELIA. why you don't call yourself a –

JO. or scrubber.

Beat.

AMELIA. Something I do, not somethin I am.

JO. You sure about that?

AMELIA. And what do you call what you are?

JO. Something he does not something I – am.

AMELIA. Somethin you are an you don't know it.

JO. Likewise.

AMELIA. Something you've become and you don't see it.

JO. I'll call you cleaner for you then, shall I?

AMELIA. Try.

JO. Or you'd prefer – ?

AMELIA. Try me.

Beat.

JO (*dryly*). Bucket isn't it?

    Then – what? You squeeze it?

    (*Amused.*) And swipe it with style.

    Well worth getting up for.

    JO *laughs a little, mockingly.*

AMELIA. I'd rather get up to that than get up to greet the
    bullshit you wake up to.

JO. . . . So would I.

AMELIA.

JO.

AMELIA. Just go, Joanne.

JO. So you've never had to check yourself?

    Never got the art of pissin quietly down pat? Cos it's all
    about technique. All bout muscles. All about muscles and
    release and flow and speed and angle – you follow me –
    you've never had to check how y'piss have ya?

    Can tell.

    And it's a little lean forward, flow against the side, little like
    pouring a good pint, little like that.

    Do someone proud.

    Flowin down quiet, smooth . . . and quiet helps. Don't it.

    Quiet is good.

    Ain't it.

    Barely audible's better.

    Isn't it.

    Helps.

    . . . Doesn't it.

    . . . *Doesn't* it? Jason

    Doesn't it?

JASON. It . . . d-d-does.

AMELIA. Does it?

JO. *Thank you.*

It was that sorta mornin.

Aye Amelia?

That's how mine was.

So. You've just been told.

AMELIA. You in no position to tell nobody nuthin though . . .

are ya.

Was yer..?

You weren't in no position to say fuck-all, is it, Jo.

Was it?

JASON (*embarrassed*). N-No.

JO. Burns me as I go and did you hear *that*?

Cos it serves me right for holding it in for so long.

Body don't like that Jay, Jay, like that ent healthy.

JASON. Ent healthy sleepin upright, you don't have to tell me and I was just about to creak me body up –

JO. I know –

JASON. when you crept back in.

JO. Post piss –

JASON. while he was asleep – and he wouldn't have known I'd been up at all would he if me body'd behaved and that was the plan and

JASON. that's the routine and

JO. that's the normal morning of it and you should know, *you* should know – I know you know what happens. I know you hear it often enough, I know you know what happens when it's not a good mornin, Jason.

JASON. And this one weren't.

JO. And I had that feelin again as I re-lay there wonderin, after I'd –

JASON. gone back into your –

JO. bedroom.

JASON. Crept back into –

JO. the bed.

JASON. Lay back down –

JO. next to him, with him deep in the land of nod.

JASON. You thought.

JO. I thought.

> *Beat.*
>
> *Beat.*
>
> . . . He's good.

AMELIA. Jason!

JO. You're good.

AMELIA. Y'shoulda –

JASON. I am aren't I Amelia?

AMELIA. shoulda – you shoulda come, come with me Jase. Shoulda seen me skating the floor dry with towels on me feet, like I do. Like I do what usedta make you laugh when you usedta see, remember.

When you usedta come, remember?

Remember when you usedta come to the caff and I usedta mop then skate and you usedta see and we usedta laugh and we was in that early together.

Remember –

JASON. when I usedta come out?

AMELIA. Remember that?

JASON. Just.

> JO *laughs a little mockingly.*

AMELIA. Skate it dry get rid a the pools of too soapy, too much, too wet mop water. Skate it dry do like my Torvill and Dean 'cept didn't know which is which which one's the woman. Who should be Torvill who should be Dean.

We never did know did we, *Jay.*

Scatting our 'Bolero' while I'm skatin it dry, singin our bad version while I'm slippin round. And you'd watch. And you'd sing.

And I'd dry skate.

And then.

I'd buff.

And you ever wondered who cleans the floors you trod daily?

JASON. You ever slept upright listenin in at a 90 degrees.

JO. You ever woke up wishin this day to be your last.

You ever wondered that?

AMELIA. *No.*

JO. You ever been up for that, Jason?

AMELIA. Leave him alone.

JO. Was up for that, was up for a morning like that.

AMELIA. Leave him alone.

JO. . . . I had that feelin again . . .

Do you see . . .

JASON. I – I can't / hear . . .

JO. It still felt like butterflies, Jason.

Felt like bad butterflies, deep down in my depths a me,
disturbin me as I lay there cold wonderin . . . . Waitin . . . .

JASON. I – I . . .

JASON *listens*

AMELIA. Jason.

JASON. What?

AMELIA. Jason!

JASON. What!?

AMELIA. JASE –

JASON. Sssshh!

JO. . . . Felt like bad butterflies going ballistic.

Felt like badness gone wrong – the insides of me carryin on
wrong like they're looking for a way out. And I felt I just
wanted to get this day started cos this new morning was
already looking old.

AMELIA. Jay.

JO. And I looked across again

JASON. and y'hubby yawned.

AMELIA. Leave Jason *alone* Jo.

JASON. I heard.

JO. And I lay there. Looking up . . .

JASON (*listening*). What –

> JO *slow rubs her belly.*
>
> JASON *listens intently.*
>
> *She slowly sighs.*
>
> *Aware, she quietly exhales.*

JO. And Jason – did you hear that?

AMELIA. That's not the point.

JO. There's only one point if you're listening in.

AMELIA. There's only one reason you're letting him listen –

JO. and you're not invited.

   . . . Do it properly, or not at all.

JASON. I will. I am.

AMELIA. Leave him outta it.

JASON. And I do.

JO. This has got nothin to do with you.

   (*Quieter.*) Listen . . .

JASON. . . . I hear him yawn –

AMELIA. he don't needta know.

JASON. Hear him yawn half awake.

AMELIA. He don't wanna know, Jo

JASON. hear him yawn and *wait.*

AMELIA. *We* don't need to know

JASON. and you're quieter, you're nervous with it, you're whisper askin

   '*Are you awake?*'

AMELIA. *'Are you awake'* – hearin you first thing – that would irritate me.

JASON. And you're askin the second time –

AMELIA. and your first time would piss me off.

JASON. And you ent even sure – but it's quieter than the first. And I'm not hearin an answer – never hear an answer

JO. cos I'm never gonna get one.

AMELIA. Just you lyin there would piss me off. Jus the you a bein you would piss me off. And I'd do you meself you lyin there irritatin like that I would. Just you bein there's more'n justification.

JASON. And you carry on with yer,

'I feel funny.'

AMELIA. That what she said?

JASON. What else?

Whisperin your – what else?

JO. *I feel hot.*

JASON. Twitchin under cover like you're restless, pull up the 12 togg a little bit higher – waitin on his move.

Waitin on his mood.

I am good at this.

Silence.

You –

JO. wait.

Pause.

JASON. Cos then you dirty dancin-belly-butterfly-come-down-burn, revealed itself as . . .

JO (*quietly*). blood.

Beat.

AMELIA. And it's not a good morning.

JASON. This is not a good morning.

JASON. This one weren't.

AMELIA. And it coulda been

JASON. but now it ent.

   And you turned it –

AMELIA. you turned it – *you* turned it

JASON. you turned it when you s-s-ss-s-

AMELIA. *said*

JO. . . . I'm bleeding.

JASON. . . . *Thass* what woke him up.

   Beat.

   Thank you.

JO.

JASON.

JO.

JASON. I creak up. Stand up to get up, getting up to get into
   position two. Second position to listen to her, better position
   to listen to yer.

   And you thought it was nerves. You thought it was s-s-
   somethin else. Your dancin – diggin

AMELIA. dirty butterfly fuckries.

JASON. The damage had been done from doing you before.

AMELIA. And from before that

JASON. burning from the inside out.

AMELIA. And from before that an' all –

JASON. burning you on their way down – and today ent even
   hardly started. And you don't haveta tell me nuthin – you
   don't tell me nuthin – you don't haveta tell me that's the
   kinda mornin it is – you don't tell me a thing cos I hear –
   heard you and you was –

JO. screaming.

JASON. And screamin like that. Like that ent healthy. J-J-Jo.

AMELIA. Screamin like that, like that ent normal Jo . . .

JO. I panicked.

JASON. And you was bleeding all / down –

JO. I – Jason –

JASON. *You* made the morning different like that –

JO. Then he –

JASON. and you was still screaming / Jo.

JO. Then he –

AMELIA. see why I left?

JO. Then he shut me up.

   Beat.

AMELIA. See why I left?

JASON. Then what did you say?

AMELIA. And who asked you to go get brave last night?

   Who asked you to brave up yourself last night and fuck up
   all a we mornin?

JO. You know what I said I don't need to repeat it, you know
   what I said – I do know you know.

JASON. This mornin, what did you say then?

AMELIA. Not so brave now are ya?

JASON. I want you to say.

JO. I know you *heard*.

   I know *what* you heard.

JASON. *Say it . . .*

JO. . . . .

AMELIA. Where's the slap-back-bitch-givin-it-the-mouth
   now?

JASON. *Say it.*

AMELIA. She for one night only then?

JO. ' . . . sorry.'

   AMELIA *shakes her head in disgust.*

AMELIA. What, sorry? – ent such a bright idea this mornin to
   raisin y'hand back at him last night is it? and is 'sorry'
   really cuttin it?

JASON. No.

No, it's not.

It wasn't.

Beat.

Thank you

Pause.

AMELIA *begins humming / half singing her tune to fill the self conscious gap.*

JO. I knew from the morning dawning that today was gonna kick.

AMELIA. Stop it.

JO. It me –

AMELIA. stop it.

JO. And it did.

I knew from the reluctant wakin, eye glue poppin, dead / leg stretching of the meeting of the . . .

AMELIA. yeh yeh yeh. You've said.

JASON. . . . But this beautiful morning's looking old and stale and worn and d-d-dirty like yesterday, already . . .

Beat.

'S lookin like you J-Jo.

JO (*mocking*). Jer-Jer-Jer-Jo.

Know you're there cos the wall shudders with yer.

JASON. Rest your head against it and I'll wh-whisper thru' in your ear.

JO. Wouldja?

JASON. . . . I did . . .

Beat.

JO. What would you wear – wondering this was your last day – start of a day like that? . . .

Beat.

AMELIA. Nothin.

Beat.

JO. I wore black to mark it.

I wore black.

Very lacy.

AMELIA. You would, you would.

JO. I did.

AMELIA. I know.

JASON. I wouldn'ta bought you that.

JO. Not old.

Not holey.

Not worn.

I wore charcoal black, bikini line BHS brand new box-fresh baggies.

And he always had taste.

AMELIA. If you like that sorta thing.

JASON. I wouldn'ta made you wear that.

JO. Thing is, that's what he brought across, 'Melia.

And that's the thing.

And that's the thing.

Things he threw across, Jason – 'cross the room at me

JASON. I heard.

JO. And he always had taste and he's fully awake and he's out from under and he's demanding me to . . . what is it – what – *what was it*, Jase..?

JASON. ' . . . get up.'

JO. Ahhh, and what do I shout back . . . *go on* . . .

JASON. ' . . . it weren't my f-f-fault.' Sorry.

JO. What do I shout back?

AMELIA. In between ya screamin.

JASON. 'It weren't my' – s– / sorry.

JO. Yeh but Jase, how do I say it without the retardation?

JASON. S-s-s– / sorry.

AMELIA. Leave him alone.

JO. And *then* what? C'mon, how good are ya?

   Don't play shy now J., cos shy don't suit –

JASON. ' . . . weren't mine neither.'

JO. weren't his what?

JASON. 'weren't mine n-neither.'

JO. Weren't his *what* neither?

JASON. ' . . . f-f– / f-f . . . '

AMELIA. *Jason!*

JO. Believe him didja?

   Say it!

AMELIA. Jo!

JASON. f-f– / f-f-

JO. Believe *him* didja?

   Say it!

JASON. F-f-fuck off.

JO. And you were gonna whisper me choice words a wisdom to help me out?

JASON. You was messin up the twelve togg.

   You was soaking through your sheets.

   You'd gone through to the m-m-mattress.

   I heard – but it weren't your fault . . . J-Jo.

   He listens.

   JO *laughs a little. Mocking.*

   And you was still screamin.

JO. I was.

JASON. You can't stop.

JO. I didn't.

AMELIA. You won't stop.

JO. I don't.

JASON. Till he stopped you.

JO. Someone had to.

JASON. Why like that?

AMELIA. Someone had to.

JASON. Why like that?

JO. *You* never saw. You only *heard*. *You* don't know.

JASON. Know what I know you make me hear –

JO. you hear what I wantcha to.

AMELIA. See.

JASON. Butcha don't know if I'm – *lis* – *l*istenin – do yer?

JO. You will. You do.

   Y'can't help yourself.

JASON. Can.

JO. Y'can't.

JASON. I can.

JO. You don't.

JASON. I could.

JO. You couldn't.

   You won't.

   I know. I know you.

   And you certainly can't help me can yer?

JASON. You-you-you –

JO. you what? You *what*! 'You! You! You!' You – *ever*?

   Is it?!

   Laughs a little. Mockingly.

   Beat.

JASON. You know if that was me with you . . . wouldn't have
   quieted you like that –

JO. that be you still being my next door knight in shining
armour. That be you still being my next door knight that
never moves a muscle that loves listenin in and whispers
words a comfort that get lost passing through. That be you
or whatever part you're wishing yourself to play in your
audio version a my mornin – Jason.

JASON. Know if that was me with you, woulda treated you

c-c-careful, Jo, gentle like – glass hearin the fragile / state
you in –

JO. you in the position that you never saw nothing though
entcha?

Didja.

You're in the position, *Jase*, that you couldn't do a thing?

Could you?

JASON. Know if that was me with you / wouldn't have –

JO. oh you would.

JASON. Woulda handled you

JO. you wouldn't.

AMELIA. I wouldn't.

JASON. Woulda treated you / gentle

JO. you couldn't.

JASON. I / could –

AMELIA. You couldn't handle that.

JO. . . .

JASON. Hearin you – / the fragile state you –

JO. You in – yeh? you – What? You in – what? – *You,* in
position (*Mocking.*) 'ter –ter–two,' Jason. Head against the
wall, pressed up hearing whatever leaks through. Jason. Is it.

Is it?

That's as good as your position two gets.

(*Mocking.*) Ger-Ger-Ger-Got.

Jason.

Isn't it?

And position three don't exist.

Does it?

Does it..?

Or, is it *that*, that makes the wall shudder with yer then.

Is it your '*position three*' that I can hear clearly comin through..?

That's when I know you're there for sure, see.

Getting your hand dirty.

Jason.

And you'd have shut me up the same way as he did . . . only you'd have been, 'positioning three' freely with it.

Jay.

This morning's as dirty as you are.

Pause.

There's a word for people like you.

AMELIA. There's a word for people like *you*.

And there is a word for people like you. Jason.

JASON. . . . There's a word for people like him and how he s-s- / shut her up –

AMELIA. didja?

JO. You ever –

AMELIA. Jason? Didja?

JASON. No.

JO. You fuckin liar –

AMELIA. Jason?

JASON. N-N-No.

JO.

JASON.

JO.

JO *and* JASON *eyeball each other challengingly. He refuses to speak on.*

(*Triumphantly.*) *Thank you.*

AMELIA.

JO.

AMELIA.

JASON *holds no eye contact.*

Beat.

Pause.

AMELIA. Bitch.

JO. And?

Beat.

Beat.

Pause.

AMELIA. Jase . . . ?

Jason . . .

JO *laughs a little at them.*

JASON. You ever pissed yourself and not known it.

You ever had to piss and not know it, done it and not realised and f-f-found out too late.

You ever done that in your adult life. Jo?

Amelia, this morning sucks.

AMELIA. This morning scares me, Jo.

JASON. You ever pissed like that?

JO. We're speaking?

JASON. I'd never pissed like that.

JO. We're speaking?

JASON. I'd never pissed like that till t-t . . . today. And I'm still shaking and you've been shut up and maybe I coulda phoned like I should, but I forgot I didn't have your number.

And maybe I regret I never called round like I could but I forgot I don't even know yer.

And I'm still next door.

And I know you knew.

And I knew you were listenin me like I listen you.

. . . And I was wet.

JO. Piss was it?

JASON. I was scared.

JO. Fear was it?

JASON. I'm wet.

JO. Wet with what tho Jase?

Wet with what?

JASON. . . . You got me been there for d-d-days

AMELIA. you got him addicted you have.

JO. Why don't you just leave?

AMELIA. You got him doin like you –

JASON. you got me not eating. Not sleeping.

You got my ear against our wall.

JO. Why don't you walk?

AMELIA. You got him hooked you have.

JO. Even to another room.

AMELIA. You got him so I don't see him.

JASON. You got me d-d-disgusted with myself daily

AMELIA. you got him where you wanted him, Jo.

JASON. Disgusting myself daily.

JO. You disgust me.

AMELIA. You got him that he don't come out.

You got him that I can't find him.

JO. Why don't you *go*?

JASON. Hourly disgusted and disgusted I'm still here and
enjoying my disgust and knowing I'll s-s– / stay.

JO. Disgusting ent it.

AMELIA. You knew he was listening –

JO. did I?

AMELIA. You knew he'd / hear –

JO. *and*?

AMELIA. *And* – you knew what you wanted him to hear,
   knowing he would stay and you knew what that would do.

JO. So?

AMELIA. So why don't *you* go?

JO. Ask *him*.

AMELIA. *Why didn't you go Jase?*

JASON. Ent that eas-eas– / easy.

JO. Ent that easy.

   Is it.

   Pause.

   You ever . . . have you..? You ever, is it. Jase?

   I think *you* have.

   Beat.

   But I left.

AMELIA. Him? I don't think so.

JO. I left.

AMELIA. Him is it?

JO. I left – the flat.

   I went.

   I went out.

JASON. You – crawled out. Jo.

   JO *quietly mouths a dry 'thank you' in* JASON's *direction.*

JO. Miss me then? What part a your anatomy missed me then?

   Beat.

   Waitin on me to apologise are ya?

   Waiting on me to apologise for getting you up are yer?

   . . . Waiting on me to apologise for keeping you up is it.

   Waiting on me to –

AMELIA. no.

JO. Are y'waiting on me to –

AMELIA. I wouldn't wait on you for nothing, Jo.

JO.

AMELIA.

JO.

JASON.

JO. What are you waiting for then?

Beat.

. . . No.

I won't apologise for it.

Thank you.

AMELIA. . . . Why did you come?

By the caff, whyja – ? And after I'd toldja not to.

After I'd asked you nice.

Whyja come? Why didja come? Why did you *come*?

JASON *starts to cry.*

JO. Did you Jason?

Beat.

Didja come?

Didja?

Beat.

Wanker.

JASON. . . . Amelia . . .

JO *watches* JASON *bemusedly.*

AMELIA *avoids his gaze.*

Amelia –

AMELIA. What?

Beat.

JASON. Ame-

AMELIA. Shhh.

Shut up.

Beat.

JO. . . . Listen.

Music track: 'Secret Place' by Jhelisa plays out.

Epilogue

Early a.m. In the moment. In the morning. In the café. The café is extremely shiny, clinically clean.

There is a large, elaborate very shiny coffee / cappuccino machine on the counter. There is an open flask on a table / chair combo, with a part-drunk flask-cup of coffee beside it.

There is a smell of yesterday's coffee about the place.

Outside it rains. It is still dark.

JO is weak. She is damaged. She is bleeding. She is wet. She is defiant. (She looks a mess.)

The tinny café radio is on, pumping out pop music (S Club 7: 'Don't Stop Movin').

AMELIA buffs her floor intensely with a cumbersome machine. (AMELIA also has 'softs' on her feet for that extra sheen.)

She gets bored.

Without looking up, AMELIA senses JO is in.

AMELIA. Get out.

JO.

AMELIA. Shut up Jo, I don't need to hear –

JO. Amelia.

AMELIA. I don't need to see . . .

JO. I'm in.

AMELIA. And we are closed.

JO.

AMELIA. Don't thank me, there's a sign.

JO. Fuck you.

AMELIA. Don't bother thank me – 'ignorant'.

JO. But I'm here now.

AMELIA. Yeh. Again. You are.

Beat.

Jesus Jo, man.

You look – a fuckin state.

JO. Thank you.

AMELIA. Y'look worse –

JO. thank you.

AMELIA. This is the worst.

JO. . . . thanks.

Beat.

AMELIA. And whatja come for?

JO. Walked.

AMELIA. Howja get here?

JO. To see you.

AMELIA. Whatja want, Jo?

JO. . . . Nuthin.

AMELIA. And 'nuthin's' got my name on it is it.

JO. –

AMELIA. 'Nuthin' happens to be where I'm at – is it.

JO. . . .

AMELIA. Again, is it? . . . Yeh?

Nothing's here for yer, is what, I toldja – is there. Is it?
Nuthin I can do yu for and – and – look at the state a yer,
y'shouldn't even be out – look how yu look nowhere near
ready to reach.

JO. But Amelia –

AMELIA. you look a fuckin state.

JO. But Amelia –

AMELIA. you got no good God reason to be out, Jo – you got no right to be out here *Jo* –

JO. see but that's the point, Amelia, now I'm in.

Be nice.

AMELIA. Nice don't getchu nowhere, does it?

JO. I wouldn't know.

AMELIA. Nice don't count for shit.

JO. I wouldn't know.

AMELIA. You wouldn't know nice if it come and smacked you round the face.

JO. It did.

AMELIA. Shit.

You seen yourself . . .

JO. 'Shit.'

AMELIA. You taken a good look?

JO. Have I?

AMELIA. Y'look . . .

JO. like I don't know.

AMELIA. . . . . You look as bad as what my floor looks good.

Looked. Good.

Look at my / floor . . .

JO. you're lookin at me like I'm lettin the side down.

AMELIA. Are ya?

JO. You're lookin at me like I'm –

AMELIA. well you tell me.

JO. Lookin / at me like –

AMELIA. look what you're doin – where you're drippin – look at my floor!

JO. Look at me.

AMELIA. No.

JO. Look at me.

AMELIA. Wha'for?

JO. Look what he / done –

AMELIA. why? Jo?

JO. Let me show you *Amelia* –

AMELIA. nah, cos – again – thank you – and – no. / So.

JO. Amelia –

AMELIA. I don't wanna see. I don't need to see. I don't have
to see – you. Yeh.

So, no.

Pause.

JO. Not this, I never.

Beat.

AMELIA. Neither did I.

Beat.

JO. Not this I wouldn't.

Beat.

AMELIA. Neither would I.

You're trouble you are, you know that.

JO. I'm here.

AMELIA. Big capital T., you know that?

JO. But I am here.

AMELIA. Big bag a double / trouble.

JO. you sound like him.

AMELIA. You look like a new sport.

JO. You've taken his lines –

AMELIA. and what have you taken? What you still takin?
What you gonna go home take more of and don't even feel
no way –

JO *just about makes to move.*

And don't sit –

JO. – down?

AMELIA. *Don't.*

JO. I won't.

AMELIA. Don't. Everything's just clean.

JO. I see.

AMELIA. Everything's just done.

JO. I know.

AMELIA. I jus done doing it all.

JO. Everything's all shiny.

AMELIA. Everything's all clean, everything's all ready. Everything's all done and prepared and washed and stacked and sparklin and ready for *them* to start *their* day, Jo, when *they* come in, and not for *you* to spoil up when *you* start yours by staggerin in here when you're ready. See.

JO. My days had started way back when.

AMELIA. My day starts because a yours.

JO. My day started / with

AMELIA. I don't wanna know.

Pause.

JO. . . . Should I shut the-?

AMELIA. That be on your way out then?

JO. . . . Should I close the / door?

AMELIA. And mark it as well? Oh no.

Beat.

AMELIA *gently, reluctantly closes the door behind* JO.

And locks it.

AMELIA *straightens up the 'closed' sign.*

This is what I'm doing from tomorrow.

This is what I shoulda done from today.

JO. I think – it'll be open.

AMELIA. From tomorrow it won't.

JO. It'll be open.

AMELIA. I'm keeping it back locked, Jo.

JO. Is it.

AMELIA. An' you can knock and knock march on up here and do what the frigg you want but I won't be opening it.

JO. Is it.

AMELIA. You'll be out. I'll be in. You'll be there. I'll be here.

In here blanking yer.

JO. What, like now?

AMELIA. Try me.

JO. I have.

AMELIA. Try me.

JO. I did.

AMELIA. Try me again.

JO. And I'm in.

See.

Beat.

AMELIA. Try me tomorrow, Joanne.

JO. . . . Won't be here then.

AMELIA. That a promise is it?

JO. Yeh.

AMELIA. Y'look shit.

AMELIA *looks to the floor at* JO's *reflection.*

Y'look shit twice.

JO *doesn't look.*

AMELIA *watches* JO, *literally dripping blood from between her legs.* JO's *dripping on the floor becomes unacceptable.*

AMELIA *exits.*

She returns with a wad of paper towels and an opened pack of sanitary towels.

AMELIA. Catch.

She gently throws the sanitary towel pack to JO, *who makes no effort to catch it. It hits her. She doesn't flinch.*

Beat.

AMELIA *starts to open up and lay paper towels un-apologetically around* JO*'s feet where she is dripping and marking the floor.*

Up close she looks at JO.

Satisfied.

JO. . . . Don't touch though.

AMELIA. Won't touch –

JO. don't touch me 'Meil. You won't –

AMELIA. I'm not.

JO. I don't want you –

AMELIA. I don't wanna – think I wanna? *Alright.*

. . . I haven't.

See.

So what am I sposed to do?

What is it I'm sposed to do?

. . . Shit.

What is it you come for?

What is it you keep coming for? What is it you want?

AMELIA *watches her bleed.*

And what's coming out?

You?

JO. Me.

AMELIA. Only you?

JO. Only me.

AMELIA *carefully lays a paper towel path towards the toilets.*

AMELIA. You sure?

Beat.

JO *nods.*

Here.

AMELIA *hands some paper towels to* JO.

Run go touch yourself.

And mind my – floor.

AMELIA *goes to hand the pack of sanitary towels to* JO.
JO *does not take them.*

And do somethin useful with these . . . y'need to sort
yourself out . . . yeh . . . fix up.

JO. Sorry about your floor.

AMELIA. So am I.

JO. Sorry bout your floor, noticed it was nice.

AMELIA. Yeh. It *was* weren't it.

JO. Sorry boutcha shine –

AMELIA. yeh – you've said.

JO. Sorry / boutcha –

    JO *is in pain.*

AMELIA. sorry boutcha self – y'need to shut up and be
    appreciated if you don't sit –

JO. can't sit –

AMELIA. (of) course.

    AMELIA *proceeds to lay a path of paper towels to a chair
    and table combo. She lays more paper towels over the table
    and over the chair.*

    Very slowly and painfully she half guides half watches JO*'s
    attempts at sitting, which is agony, but eventually
    successful.*

    This is part routine for both of them.

JO. You done something different then? You've done somethin
    nice for 'em? Is this some occasion? You gone that extra
    mile have you? – you have, you've pushed the boat out to
    make a good impression, trying t' get in their good books –

or just to stay there – what is it – you get a gold star or something for how much shine the floor's showing? . . .

Notice things like that I do.

S'a woman's eye.

Detail. Got the eye for it. You and me both.

Notice things like that don't we.

Bet they won't.

Beat.

I'm impressed.

Beat.

Did I say that I was impressed?

Beat.

What you do's impressive.

And least you're gettin outta your house.

AMELIA. Least I am.

JO. Least you got somewhere to go.

AMELIA. Least I have.

JO. . . . Least you got that.

AMELIA *sits and sips from her (flask) coffee.*

JO *watches.*

AMELIA *offers.*

No.

AMELIA *drinks.*

Thirsty though.

AMELIA. I don't do service.

JO. Cuppa somethin warm 'n' wet. All milk and froth –

AMELIA. don't do service do I.

I won't do service.

JO. Still not allowed to touch their stuff?

Still wishin you could?

AMELIA. Still wishin you weren't here – still wishin you'd fuck off –

JO. I'm thirsty.

AMELIA. Least a your worries.

JO. I want a drink.

AMELIA. Little thirst ent gonna hurtcha.

JO. It does though

AMELIA. 'll blend in with the rest then won't it.

Beat.

JO. I'm not beggin it for free.

I wouldn't do that. I wouldn't do that would I?

AMELIA. You playing proud now?

JO. I wouldn't know.

AMELIA. God don't like proud.

JO. God don't like ugly.

AMELIA. Keep going . . .

JO. God don't like me.

AMELIA. Nah, it's – I who don't like you, Jo.

JO. There you go sounding like him again, Amelia.

. . . Go on . . .

AMELIA. They'll be in to open up soon.

JO. Go on . . . I know you know how.

Beat.

AMELIA. They got their own little coffee machine routines.

JO. Go on. I know you wanna.

AMELIA. Their own little ways a doin it.

JO. Impress me.

AMELIA. . . . Stand there and do the noises sometimes, don't I. Style it out my way. Stand there and do the noises and make like I even got a queue an' everything.

Sometimes.

When I'm on me own. In on me own. Here.

Do it how I seen it been done, how I seen them do it, make like I'm all stressed like how they do. Cept I'd do it better. And I watch 'em from the sly – from the outside in – when my shift's over when daylight hits and the daytime people come in and do their thing.

When I'm here on me own.

Make out like it's the lunchtime rush and I'm dealin with it single handed – on me jack – and there's a little bit a the 'queue-rage' goin down that I'm tryinta pacify and I'm imaginin pumpin out cups a 'this' – take out 'that's' – grande whatevers and –

Beat.

sometimes I piss about like that.

Fuck about like that.

Fucked ent it.

JO.

AMELIA.

JO.

AMELIA. . . . When they come, Jo, when they open up, I'm gonna go. Gonna go back home, I'm gonna skip up my stairs, gonna visit my bedroom, gonna turn off my radio – I'm gonna – might even take a little *lie* down – Jo, gonna turn everything off and take this as the 'quiet' it is while I know you're out and about.

AMELIA *makes to clean up some of the paper towels on the floor. She doesn't notice that she has* JO*'s blood on her own feet so every step makes a bloody footprint.*

She becomes part of her own problem.

JO. You really make the coffee machine noises with your mouth, fakin it . . . ?

AMELIA.

JO.

AMELIA.

JO. Do yer? I think that's cute that is.

Really. I do.

(*Dryly.*) I think that's really . . . *somethin –*

JO *suddenly vomits over the floor, where there are no paper towels.*

AMELIA. Jesus Jo, man.

AMELIA *notices her own prints.*

What's the matter with you?

JO. Uhhh . . .

. . . I'll be alright.

AMELIA. Oh Jesus.

Shit.

JO. I will –

AMELIA. shit.

JO. I'll be fine –

AMELIA. *fuck.* / Jo.

JO. Thanks.

I'm OK.

Did I say I was sorry boutcha floor?

I am.

AMELIA. Fuck you Jo –

JO. I really am and 'don't thank me' –

AMELIA. and fuck him too . . . y'need to stay – y'need to stay – y'need to stay away, away from me – from me, from Jase, from me, from here.

From him. Fuck you Jo.

You need to stay away and I am gonna keep the door locked back from tomorrow

JO. won't matter won't be here then.

AMELIA. Y'said that yesterday –

JO. you ever woke up wonderin this was / your last day

AMELIA. said that the day before an' all.

JO. This one's it.

AMELIA. You're gonna haveta keep away.

JO. Today is it.

AMELIA. You're gonna haveta keep your distance.

JO. This has to be it

AMELIA. cos I'll be keeping mine.

JO. I want this to be it

AMELIA. but you'll be back though.

You'll be back, Jo.

You'll be back here –

JO. this is it

AMELIA. cos you *go* back.

Cos you do.

So, we're fucked.

Beat.

JO. . . . I want this day to be over.

AMELIA. And I'm askin you nice.

JO. Want this day to be over –

AMELIA. I'm sayin it *nice* –

JO. need this mornin to finish.

AMELIA. I am bein nice.

And I'm not gonna be able to ask you nicely again am I?

AMELIA *draws a clean glass of crisp water*

JO. Not what I want.

Not what I want.

It's not what I want.

She gives it to JO.

I won't drink it.

AMELIA. . . . I know thatcha will.

JO. I won't.

AMELIA. I know thatcha will. I know you tho.

JO. . . . I know you more.

AMELIA. And I know you more'n that, don't I.

JO.

AMELIA.

JO. This mornin ent had nuthin good to offer up, y'know? It
started off shit – y'know? – and it don't finish yet and I
can't wait for the afternoon to come.

Music track: 'Secret Place' starts to build.

JO *drinks.*

AMELIA. Jesus.

JO. I can't wait.

I proper can't wait.

AMELIA. Jo?

JO. Amelia . . .

AMELIA. Jo . . .

Jo –

JO. Sshh.

Music track 'Secret Place' continues to play out.

End.

A Nick Hern Book

dirty butterfly first published in Great Britain in 2003 as a paperback
original by Nick Hern Books Limited, 14 Larden Road, London
W3 7ST, in association with the Soho Theatre, London

Reprinted 2008

Cover image: Discalfani/Paul Beard/Getty Images

Typeset by Country Setting, Kingsdown, Kent CT14 8ES
Printed in the UK by CPI Antony Rowe, Chippenham, Wiltshire

A CIP catalogue record for this book is available from the British Library

ISBN 978 1 85459 741 0